Playtime Ball Sports

written by Anne Giulieri

illustrated by Cherie Zamazing

There are lots of ball games that you can play at school.

Here are three games for you to try.

They are: **Down Ball, Wall Pat** and **Toe-touch Catchy.**

Anyone can play these games!

Down Ball

To play Down Ball you need two *squares* and a ball.
The squares can be marked with *chalk* on the ground.

Ask a friend to stand in one square
and you can stand in the other square.

When you are ready, *bounce* the ball
into your friend's square.
Your friend must try to tap the ball back
into your square as quickly as they can.
You both need to be careful
that you only let the ball bounce once.

Down Ball is just like a game of Catch
but you don't *catch* the ball — you tap it.
If you miss the ball, you have to start the game again.
Sometimes you can play with four friends
and four squares.

Wall Pat

Wall Pat is lots of fun.
You only need a wall and a ball!

Here is how to play.
Stand a little bit away from a wall.
Pat the ball down with your hand once,
so it bounces and then hits the wall.
As the ball bounces back,
catch it or just pat it back again.

Toe-touch Catchy

You can play Toe-touch Catchy anywhere at school.
All you need is a friend and a ball.

To play Toe-touch Catchy, you need to stand near
your friend, so that your toes *touch*!

The first thing you do is *throw* the ball to your friend.
You should be good at doing this
when you are near your friend.
But when you get far away, it will be tricky to do!

Every time you catch the ball,
take one little step *backwards* and throw the ball again.
Do this every time you catch the ball.

Don't drop the ball!
If you drop it, you must go back to the start
and touch toes again.
Try it! It's fun!

What ball games do you play at school?

14

Picture Glossary

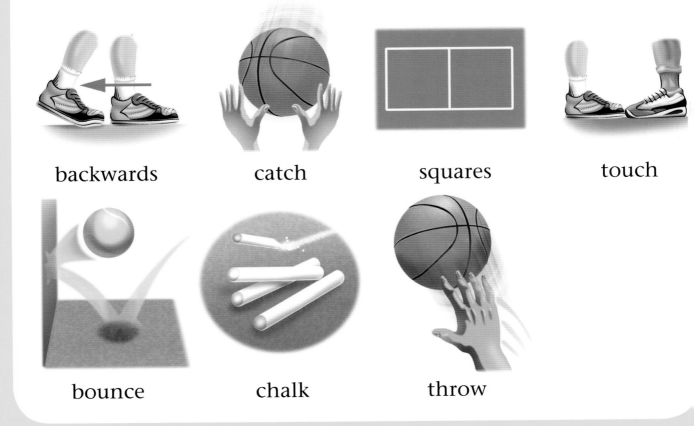

backwards

catch

squares

touch

bounce

chalk

throw